Self-Esteem

The Introductory Manual For Cultivating And Overseeing
Relationships, Comprehending Others, Enhancing
Self-Assurance, And Refining Social Skills

*(The Definitive Manual For Enhancing Self Esteem And
Cultivating Robust Self Assurance)*

Gene Harrington

TABLE OF CONTENT

Achieving Your Goals 1

Maximizing Introversion 14

Self-Esteem And Self-Confidence 39

Why Do Goals Fail To Yield Results For The Majority Of Individuals? 51

Place Confidence In Your Own Emotions 58

You Are What You Eat 74

The Influence Of Optimistic Thought Patterns 80

Become More Self-Aware 99

Uncovering The Sources Of Personal Motivation: A Guide 125

Achieving Your Goals

You are cultivating a sense of self-assurance, thereby enabling yourself to express your thoughts confidently and assertively to your superiors, illustrating your presence and exceptional value as an employee You will find it satisfactory to acknowledge and accept the recognition you rightfully deserve for your diligent efforts. Upon entering the office, your confident gait and posture will inevitably capture the attention of those present.

Prior to delving too deeply into the task of enhancing your self-esteem, it is crucial to recognize that there exists an equilibrium between exhibiting excessive confidence and being excessively reticent. You aspire to be positioned at a moderate midpoint. It is acceptable to acknowledge one's own accomplishments and it is appropriate to gracefully accept the recognition one rightfully deserves. It can be rather irksome and at times even impolite to ostentatiously display oneself, akin to a peacock, while boasting about one's own achievements to anyone willing to lend an ear. A suitable term for that behavior exists—arrogant. Displaying arrogance implies that one has overstepped boundaries and would benefit from exercising restraint. Arrogance will not win you any friends and will ultimately cost you a few along with any respect you have earned.

Having self-assurance is a necessity for achieving success. The attainment of your goals will remain elusive unless you commence the cultivation of self-confidence without delay. One must possess a belief in their abilities before achieving success. Certainly, there may be some reservations that arise when one establishes the objective of achieving an 'A' on their term paper or securing a promotion. Nevertheless, deep down, you possess the self-assurance and conviction that you possess the necessary capabilities to accomplish these aims.

Without sufficient self-assurance, one will perpetually refrain from pursuing their objectives, often leading to an incapacity to establish any ambitions. You may find yourself mired in a cycle of stagnation, steadily plunging into a realm of despondency due to your circumstances. Nevertheless, the repercussions of not taking any action far exceed the potential consequences of making an attempt and not succeeding.

What is the significance of possessing a strong sense of self-assurance in order to effectively accomplish one's objectives?

-You will have the courage to try, to start something new and uncertain.

- You will develop sufficient self-belief to advance towards a goal.

- You will possess the motivation and determination requisite for achieving success.

- You are entitled to decline opportunities that do not appeal to your preferences or prove to be unproductive in order to effectively manage your time.

- The presence of your self-assurance will effectively eradicate the apprehension that impedes your progress.

- One may choose to embrace a positive response when faced with an exhilarating prospect instead of succumbing to apprehension stemming from uncertainty.

- Your unwavering self-assurance allows you to establish ambitious objectives that will pave the way for remarkable accomplishments, rather than settling for meager goals that yield minimal triumph.

- You have the ability to diplomatically assert yourself and demand the respect that you are entitled to, showcasing your finesse.

Be committed

Nevertheless, perhaps your diminished self-assurance has placed you at a slight disadvantage in the realm of verbal presentations. We shall designate this trait as a vulnerability of yours. You possess satisfactory organizational abilities, however, your aptitude for generating reports is exceptional, and the supervisor has already conveyed his satisfaction with your extensive expertise. You are fortunate to have a colleague who possesses exemplary public speaking skills, as well as another colleague who has attained a high level of proficiency in organizational abilities.

Not all individuals are suited for the art of public speaking. Worrying about your incapacity to address a gathering with the same ease as conversing with a close confidant is an exercise in futility. It is possible for you to make minor enhancements in this regard; nevertheless, without possessing the inherent abilities of a skilled orator, your mastery of public speaking may never truly reach a level of polished finesse. This does not imply that you are incapable or undeserving of the promotion. Seek guidance from your colleague and observe their performance to gain valuable insights. Please request assistance from your colleague in organizing and cleaning your workstation. This will instill a sense of worth in them, while also presenting an opportunity for one to acquire knowledge from individuals who possess distinct capabilities.

You can demonstrate a strong commitment to your work and leave a positive impression on your boss by consistently arriving punctually and consistently submitting exceptional reports. Direct some focus towards improving your organizational aptitude while dedicating the majority of your efforts and resources towards enhancing the quality of your statements. Such is the caliber of your abilities, which will undoubtedly lead to your well-deserved promotion.

The advantages of employing affirmative self-dialogue

Possibly the most profound influence we can employ to maximize our personal advantage in life is self.

Particularly, we can employ our contemplations as they have an influence on our emotions and thus

Lines have the potential to significantly impact our overall approach to life. Through the development of effective methods to regulate our

Alterations should be made to the internal dialogues, converting self-talk from negative to positive, rather than succumbing to pessimistic tendencies, a tendency displayed by the majority.

The majority of individuals, often without conscious awareness, engage in this practice throughout the course of the day, allowing them to effectively address various aspects of their lives.

and implement fundamental enhancements.

Your ability to succeed in life greatly depends on your approach to life, a positive mindset being crucial.

A positive and focused mindset fosters a confident and ultimately more successful individual than one overflowing.

characterized by a pessimistic outlook, inducing a lack of courage and diminished self-assurance. By adopting a positive mindset, one adopts a different perspective towards life, contrasting with a mindset of negativity.

Having an inspirational mindset encourages us to perceive greatness in both individuals and the world, thereby leading to

Exemplary integrity and notable accomplishments. Your personal contentment is contingent upon your thoughts and emotions.

With each passing moment, and by altering the way in which you perceive, you can significantly transform your perspective.

Existence and effectively navigate through one's daily affairs.

One who approaches life with a positive mindset is more prepared for the challenges that may come their way.

Effectively navigate the challenges that life presents, individuals possess the resilience to rebound and recover.

due to challenges or strategic maneuvers encountered in various aspects of life. The person with idealistic tendencies will perceive

The reality regarding the matter is that it is merely a temporary setback from which they can recover and move forward.

By adopting an optimistic perspective, the individual can assume complete control over their life.

their deliberations and sentiments and turn an adverse situation into a progressively favorable one.

One could generate a positive outcome by essentially modifying their cognitive patterns. Since contemplations can

You may either be certain or hold a contrasting perspective, with the capacity to maintain only one concept as the utmost focus at any given moment.

At that juncture, opting for a constructive mindset will enable you to maintain a positive orientation in your thoughts, emotions, and behaviors, ultimately resulting in a happier individual who is better equipped to accomplish their objectives with greater ease.

Incorporating optimistic self-dialogue into your everyday routines

Throughout the entirety of the day, it is advisable to engage in the practice of employing positive self-dialogue in order to establish a fresh mindset.

For instance, it is highly probable that you have amassed a substantial body of evidence for negative inference over a prolonged duration and

Enduring through this will require time and effort. Initially, one must anticipate the practice of consistently engaging in positive self-talk multiple times throughout the day. This can be accomplished by repeatedly reciting...

Utter affirmations quietly to oneself or audibly, employing discretion. Positive self-talk

can be employed for a broad spectrum of applications throughout the course of your lifetime, it has the potential to aid you in surmounting

In challenging circumstances, instill self-confidence within yourself, assist in breaking habits, and facilitate healing.

Attain a quicker recovery from ailment or implement modifications to your overall lifestyle. are well-known or widely recognized" "renowned phrases or sentences that have achieved widespread acclaim" "notable sayings or sentences that have garnered significant recognition" "prominent expressions or sentences that have gained considerable fame"

May be employed in the practice of incorporating positive internal dialogue.

- I am faced with a captivating challenge - this can be employed in instances of problem occurrence.

In the course of our daily existence or in the presence of adversity, rather than merely observing the surrounding circumstances

viewing the situation in a pessimistic way and perceiving it as a problem, regarding it as a challenge

significantly more constructive approach for handling the situation.

- I have a positive self-perception, which can be leveraged to cultivate confidence and enhance self-esteem.

reflect upon oneself and the person one is, similar assertions could be "I contemplate my own being and the individual that I am"

"I excel at what I do", "I possess admirable qualities", or "I am a person of integrity and merit".

I understand that I am capable of accomplishing this - this option can be employed when you are confronted with

preliminary assessment to determine your suitability for a particular endeavor

pose a challenge for me\\\" in a more formal tone."

pose a concern for me"

- I am filled with a robust sense of health, energy, and vitality – this can be harnessed for empowerment.

thoughtful expressions regarding your welfare either following a period of incapacitation or during

Undergoing a period of convalescence following an illness.

- I am content as an individual, and this can be harnessed to promote overall positive thoughts about oneself and the world in which one resides.

Maximizing Introversion

A multitude of individuals exhibiting introverted tendencies experience a persistent sense of displacement in various settings, particularly within the workplace, public domains, and occasionally when among a collective. The issue at hand pertains to individuals who dominate conversations or elicit the most laughter, thereby hindering meaningful discourse. Communicating with others and forming genuine connections is a challenge, as many individuals lack proficiency in humor. Frequently, prior to their inclusion in group discussions or work meetings, individuals are often preconceived as the "solitary" type - reserved, timid, and occasionally perceived as being anti-social. This societal stigma further exacerbates the challenges faced by individuals who value solitude, impeding their ability to effectively integrate into social dynamics or advance in their professional careers. They are increasingly understanding that achievement is exclusively suited to individuals who possess the ability to confidently captivate an audience and assertively execute novel concepts. Prepare yourself, as significant changes are on the horizon.

With the increase in introspective individuals' awareness of the somewhat privileged statuses of extroverted personalities, they are concurrently acknowledging that their introversion does not constitute any form of disadvantage. It is, in reality, an exceedingly efficient tool and untapped resource accessible solely to those of a reserved nature, serving as an advantage to introverts. The labor force is the primary context in which each productive member of society dedicates a significant portion of their daily activities. The taciturn individuals possess distinctive inherent talents that enable them to effectively capitalize on the situation, thus leaving no justification for them not to make the most out of it.

Overcome Shyness

The reserved individuals may not necessarily possess a phobia of engaging in conversations with individuals beyond their social circle, but it is not uncommon to observe traces of shyness in a few of them. To some you are indeed shy, overcoming it is a task they must face first. Contrary to the general populace, introverted individuals do not find it favorable to be thrust into social settings and rely on trial and error as a means of learning. Moreover, they do not exhibit positive response to coercion or intimidation tactics employed for the purpose of motivation. For those who are reticent, this can be perceived as a type of aggression and a further validation of why individuals deplete their vitality. The optimal approach to addressing shyness entails fostering understanding among introverts regarding the given circumstances. The inquiries of reasons behind and reasons against must be addressed.

Why should you speak? Because you have ideas. Indeed, there exist superior concepts that can further the objectives of the company without entailing excessive risks. Your objective is not to seek admiration or praise from others, but rather to actively participate in the professional arena and receive due recognition for your valuable contributions. Have you ever encountered a situation where you declined to express your thoughts, only for the governing entity to select an idea that was significantly inferior to what you had proposed? Is the phrase "My proposal was of superior quality" recognizable to you? Not only was this ill-advised endeavor carried out, but its vague conception and inherent risk subsequently had a detrimental effect on the collective effort, including your own. The environment is characterized by a raucous commotion that may prove excessively stimulating for individuals who are introverted. Should you choose not to vocalize your thoughts for the purpose of gaining acknowledgment, I urge you to express yourself with the intention of mitigating the disarray that impinges upon your ability to focus and engage in solitary pursuits.

Interacting with individuals can evoke apprehension in certain individuals due to the potential for conversations to transition seamlessly from one subject to another, thus giving rise to informal discourse. Chats are small talks. Casual conversations swiftly transition and can encompass a wide range of topics. It is expected that all individuals shall strive to catch up and actively contribute their insights on various subjects. Introverted individuals encounter difficulty in navigating this process. In addition to requiring time for thoughtful contemplation, their access to office news or gossip is exceedingly restricted. However, interpersonal communication serves as the attenuating factor in the manifestation of shyness.

Talk about work. Engage in a direct and personal interaction with a fellow professional within the workplace. The context holds significant importance as it conveys the message that the discussion revolves around your ongoing projects and the means through which he can offer assistance. Discussing the job would be beneficial for you, as an introvert, as it would provide you with an in-depth understanding of the job's nature, enabling you to effortlessly respond to any related inquiries. It additionally diminishes the likelihood of engaging in casual conversation. This scenario offers you the opportunity to have control over the conversation, which is unlike the case in a group meeting where the flow can originate from any or all directions, leading to a sense of being overwhelmed. It is imperative that you maintain this sense of control.

At this junction, you might be pondering the strategies for effectively addressing an audience. Never fear. You simply need to recollect the feeling of mastery that you acquired during your individual dialogue. It might come as a surprise to learn that introverts find one-on-one conversations to be particularly challenging. In contrast, delivering a speech before an audience is a relatively effortless endeavor. Why, you ask. The management of the circulation. When engaging in verbal communication, you possess the ability to dictate or regulate the tempo at which the conversation progresses. You have the freedom to proceed at a leisurely pace without fear of interruption or being subjected to trivial conversations. Given your expertise in the subject matter being discussed, individuals may pose inquiries, to which you would possess instant and comprehensive responses. It falls within the realm of your authority while they assume the role of mere observers. It confers an advantage upon introverts.

Continue to engage in activities that have been proven to be effective.
The success of individuals who exhibit introverted traits relies on their adept utilization of their inherent abilities to thrive. It is widely acknowledged that introverts gain knowledge primarily

through observation, possess the ability to make astute judgments uninterrupted, and exhibit productivity while working in solitude. They flourish in an environment devoid of incessant office noise. While some individuals are content with merely observing the surface level of a notion, the reserved and thoughtful individuals delve deeper and persistently pursue its thorough understanding. This is a highly valued attribute that employers attach significance to, thus it is essential to optimize its potential.

Steve Wozniak appears to be an ardent advocate of the merits of solitude and independent work. In his modest office space at Hewlett Packard, he spearheaded the development of the Apple computer, a technological breakthrough that revolutionized the field of computing. Up to this point, he has been placing considerable emphasis on the notion that innovation is seldom accomplished within a collective setting. He has a point. Isolation is not limited to those who are naturally reticent. It serves as a means of shielding oneself from the cacophonous environment. It provides them with an optimal setting that is conducive to the way their cognitive processes operate. In the absence of disturbances, their cognitive processes remain undisturbed, thereby enhancing their productivity.

Work alone. Keep doing that. As an individual with introverted tendencies, you may often find yourself with numerous thoughts that require articulation in a manner comprehensible to others. Instances of disturbances and breaks in continuity inhibit the smooth progression of cognitive processes, necessitating their avoidance. Engaging in solitude is a pleasurable undertaking for individuals who are reserved by nature. Consequently, while fulfilling your duties, you are simultaneously experiencing enjoyment. It is these serendipitous occurrences in life that have the potential to contribute to the success of an introvert. This should not be interpreted as grounds for the elimination of collaboration in a professional setting. Research has consistently demonstrated that greater achievements have been attained through individual efforts as opposed to collective endeavors. It constitutes more of an earnest request to permit employees to seek solace in their personal domains whenever necessary. Isolation has the potential to act as a catalyst for exceptional performance.

It is unnecessary to remind you to prioritize singular tasks, as you have likely been adhering to this practice consistently. Keep doing it. It should not be inferred as sluggish, but rather as meticulous. You allocate the workload into digestible segments, address and comprehend each of them, and devise resolutions. Evaluate the optimal solution by assessing the potential risks and returns. This method offers an ideal means of comprehending the assigned tasks, enabling you to confidently address any inquiries during meetings without being caught off guard. Any reputable employer will consistently prioritize the caliber of their employees' work as opposed to its volume.

Acquire knowledge proportionately to your efforts. This task should pose no difficulty, as individuals who are introverted often derive great enjoyment from engaging in extensive reading. Keep doing it. Perpetual learning shall forever remain an integral facet within an introvert's realm. It serves as a source of exhilaration for numerous individuals, and more importantly, it constitutes a pivotal instrument for achieving success. The potential utility of even the simplest piece of information may forever elude one's comprehension. However, when the opportune moment arises, you possess the assurance and comprehensive resources necessary. The realm of introverts may potentially serve as an ideal environment for honing one's skills and acquiring readiness for various circumstances.

3.1 Enhancing Your Emotional Intelligence: Strategies for Improvement

Prior to engaging in advanced critical thinking, it is imperative that one possesses a comprehensive understanding of oneself. There exist various approaches through which one can effectively structure their thought process in this particular domain. One approach to consider is the utilization of VITALS as a method. VITALS is an acronym denoting values, interests, temperament, around-the-clock availability, life mission, and strengths.

Allow us to delve into the utilization of VITALS as a method for examining one's own self within various categories. The initial classification pertains to your "values." It is imperative to assess your life's driving forces in order to discern the presence of your values in previous choices. Perhaps you have placed a high importance on your physical well-being, and devoted substantial time to maintaining a state of good physical condition. This holds considerable value. Another may be family. Have you maintained strong familial bonds and fostered a robust communication framework with your relatives? It is possible that you may have placed excessive significance on certain matters. Perhaps you have dedicated excessive amounts of time towards the pursuit of wealth or amorous companionship. This region exhibits a strong correlation with motivation. For individuals seeking to maintain their motivation and stay on course, it is essential to acknowledge their core values and strive to prioritize and integrate them into both their professional and personal endeavors.

The subsequent classification pertains to "interests." While closely connected to values, it exhibits a slight distinction. Interests refer to the categories of activities or subjects that individuals prefer to pursue. This may encompass personal interests, issues, or fervors. Certain individuals perceive that they are incapable of pursuing a livelihood as a professional artist, but engaging in the leisurely pursuit of painting aids them in establishing emotional stability, fostering well-being, and cultivating an enhanced emotional consciousness. Certain individuals have the capacity to derive a livelihood from their personal passions. These could encompass a diverse array of objects or concepts. Possible alternative: "Possible areas of interest encompass political objectives, civic engagement, or interpersonal dynamics."

The subsequent classification pertains to the aspect of "temperament," encompassing the characterization of one's inherent disposition and predilections. Would you consider yourself to lean more towards introversion or extroversion? In which circumstances do you experience the greatest sense of ease and comfort? This might require an examination of your social connections and their composition. Certain individuals have a propensity for engaging in impromptu activities. On occasions when they chance upon a restaurant they have yet to experience, they may spontaneously opt to give it a try, by way of illustration. Certain individuals will consistently opt not to engage in such a course of action and instead continue to bypass the restaurant, unless a prior appointment to visit the establishment is arranged.

The abbreviation "A" signifies the term "around-the-clock," which pertains to one's biorhythms. Biorhythm is a concept that pertains to the inherent physiological or biological processes that humans engage in, and the synchronization of these functions with time-dependent patterns. Sleeping illustrates the manifestation of biorhythm, as it typically commences at approximate nightly intervals (if one is fortunate) and ideally concludes at consistent daytime intervals. Our biorhythms facilitate a profound interconnectedness with the world. The rotation of the earth exerts an influence on our physical beings, ultimately tethering us to its all-encompassing cadence. All-encompassing monitoring of your sexual behaviors, dietary patterns, physical activities, and other physiological processes on a continuous basis. Examining these functions in our lives with great scrutiny can potentially enhance our comprehension regarding the manner in which we structure our existence.

Understanding oneself may initially appear to be an uncomplicated endeavor. It could potentially be more intricate than anticipated. When conducting a thorough self-evaluation and analysis of your decisions, endeavor to identify the aspects in which you are notably vulnerable. It is also essential to recognize and acknowledge your areas of expertise. Indeed, upon scrutinizing your life, you may uncover that you are either an individual who excessively focuses on their strengths or someone who excessively fixates on their weaknesses. Should you be someone inclined towards fixating on your strengths, you may discover that you possess a diminished capacity to discern areas of weakness or relative inadequacy in comparison to others. Individuals displaying such a propensity are inclined towards narcissism. They often need to cultivate a greater sense of selflessness. This individual exhibits self-appreciation, which is admirable, yet they lack the capacity to provide themselves with constructive self-assessment regarding areas in need of personal growth.

The alternative category of individuals lacks the capacity to observe and acknowledge their own inherent capabilities. They excessively direct their attention to their shortcomings and harbor the belief that they lack the merit or adequacy to receive commendation. They should exhibit a greater degree of self-prioritization. These two categories of individuals exemplify distinct perspectives on self-centeredness. The suffix "ish" denotes a semantic significance, indicating possession or conformity to a particular manner or characteristic. To exhibit selfishness entails possessing autonomy over oneself, exhibiting an inward focus, and exerting self-governance. This term is frequently associated with unfavorable implications; however, it encourages one to perceive it as a matter of impartial significance. Selfishness essentially entails a preoccupation with one's own interests and desires. While it is undeniable that certain individuals ought to exhibit less selfishness, it is equally important to acknowledge that numerous individuals will need to cultivate a greater sense of self-interest. These individuals were informed that they were undeserving of any form of entitlements. These individuals lack the ability to maintain a suitable level of self-interest and often allow others to take advantage of them. In the process of self-discovery, it is imperative to bear the following consideration in mind. Conduct a thorough examination of your life to identify any indications of an inequitable distribution of self-centeredness, whether leaning towards excessive self-interest or its opposite.

This proposition is intended for individuals who are inclined to enhance their discernment of non-verbal communication and seek to do so with a sense of gravity. Acquire a pair of musical instruments that you and a companion, associate, or collaborator can employ collectively. This ought to be a pursuit characterized by relaxation and leisure. Extend an invitation to another individual to partake in your activities and collectively make observations. It is advisable to commence by establishing a consistent beat to maintain the tempo; however, as you gain proficiency and ease, you may gradually immerse yourself in the rhythm and venture into experimental techniques. One can derive significant benefit merely from establishing a rhythm for others to adhere to and providing them with support within that rhythm.

Alternatively, you could consider experimenting with the guitar or piano to further expand your skillset. The aforementioned approach can be implemented similarly, by engaging in the activity alongside an individual proficient in drums or other percussion instruments. This particular activity diverges slightly in terms of non-verbal communication techniques, as engaging in it independently entails communicating with oneself in the absence of a practice partner. Although this is acceptable, it does not contribute to fostering a reciprocal form of communication, transforming it into a one-sided endeavor akin to personal journaling or engaging in artistic pursuits independently.

Music is regarded as a highly refined means of non-verbal correspondence. This particular aspect of the communication medium stands out due to its integration of auditory and visual elements, akin to verbal discourse, yet distinctly devoid of written or spoken language, save for the inclusion of lyrical content. The integration of lyrical content poses a complex challenge within the encompassing aesthetics of this composition. The lyrics encompass written language, distinct from oral communication, and thus possess the remarkable ability to undergo a profound transformation of significance when conveyed through musical rendition. Therefore, they are not regarded as verbal communication in the conventional understanding of language.

The music, nevertheless, prevails as an enigmatic mode of communication within our repertoire. Music possesses the ability to be deeply infused with emotion, despite the fact that its composition is a nuanced and unconventional art form. Despite years of dedicated practice and extensive study, individuals may still find themselves unable to make notable improvements in their musical abilities. This exemplifies the extent of disparities present in the diverse languages of music across the globe. In addition to the existence of distinct musical languages, there also exists a variety of musical dialects. Music serves as a comprehensive conduit for communication and expression, capable of conveying both ordinary and profound messages that originate from the depths of one's being.

Music is comprised of frequencies, which serve as quantifications of the oscillations produced by acoustic waves resulting from ongoing events. The sense of hearing serves as a profoundly personal link between individuals, and it is widely known that music has the potential to elicit profound and long-forgotten recollections in individuals affected by Alzheimer's or dementia. This phenomenon occurs due to the profound interconnection between music and our perception of the world, as sound permeates every facet of our experiences. Sound assumes equal significance alongside the senses of taste, sight, touch, and smell. It serves as a fundamental means through which we can maintain connectivity with the global community. Music frequently incorporates visual elements, particularly when observed in a live performance; the auditory aspect truly serves as the binding agent to one's emotions.

If an individual were to attend a symphony orchestra performance and query each member of the audience about their respective experience upon its culmination, a multitude of diverse responses would invariably emerge. Certain individuals may assert that its aesthetic allure was of a remarkable magnitude, and they experienced a captivating sense of awe in light of the orchestra's astounding prowess. Certain individuals may express the perspective that they perceived the work as tragic, evoking feelings of sadness during certain segments. Alternative phrasing in a formal tone: Some individuals may assert that the impact on them was negligible and that they held little regard for the performance. An individual lacking a response in response to your query may resort to fabricating false information.

This serves as a demonstration of the inherent capacity of music to offer profound experiences to individuals and its remarkable power to evoke emotions and provoke contemplation within each and every one of us. This is non-verbal communication.

Additionally, one could emphasize that verbal communication exhibits a similar disparity. During an oral communication presentation, if you were to survey the same audience following a speech or lecture, it is likely that you would receive equally detached responses. Certain individuals would effectively summarize the key points, while others may lack the ability to articulate the events that transpired. Instead of focusing on the substance, certain individuals may offer their perspective on the delivery of the oration. The cognitive interpretation of content cannot be accurately quantified.

Self-Esteem And Self-Confidence

In the introductory section, we briefly addressed the fundamental elements of self-esteem and underscored its significant value. Incorporated within this chapter, we shall also delve into the acquisition of knowledge regarding self-assurance. Self-confidence is frequently mistaken for self-esteem due to their similarities in sound, despite their fundamental disparity in definition. According to the definition provided in the Oxford dictionary, self-confidence can be described as a sense of reliance on one's own capabilities, attributes, and discernment. Diverging from the concept of self-esteem, self-confidence pertains specifically to an individual's performance and how it instills within them the assurance to persist in their endeavors or embark on novel ventures.

When an individual possesses greater self-assurance in their aptitude to execute tasks or actions, they are inclined to experience a heightened sense of contentment as a result of more frequent achievements. When an individual possesses faith in their own abilities, they are driven to undertake the necessary actions required to accomplish their aspirations. Self-assurance places significant emphasis on an individual's positive evaluation of their prior achievements, thus bestowing upon them the ability to enhance their forthcoming endeavors.

Similar to self-esteem, self-confidence may be a concept that presents challenges in terms of complete comprehension. It is imperative that we possess a precise understanding of the concept of self-confidence before proceeding any further, given that it will be extensively employed throughout the content of this book. Presented below are several illustrative instances that will aid in enhancing comprehension of the concept of self-confidence:

- An individual has the capacity to recognize and appreciate their inherent worth irrespective of their past errors.

- It is possible for individuals to maintain a positive self-image and acknowledge their worth despite their flaws.

- An individual exhibits the courage to advocate for themselves and assert their opinions.

- An individual possesses the awareness that they are entitled to companionship and admiration from their peers.

- An individual possesses complete self-awareness and demonstrates the capacity to embrace all aspects of their character, encompassing both their strengths and weaknesses.

Self-confidence does not encompass the following qualities/characteristics:

• An individual maintaining the belief in their own perfection or striving towards an ideal of perfection.

• An individual who sets unattainable standards and expectations for themselves

• An individual who is endeavoring to attain a life devoid of hardships, suffering, and challenges.

• An individual who exhibits a pronounced egocentricity and prioritizes their own objectives and requirements.

When individuals initially acquaint themselves with the concept of self-confidence, a common misconception arises wherein individuals erroneously conflate it with tunnel vision. In this state, individuals solely prioritize their own needs and aspirations, aiming to attain a more seamless and effortless existence. While it is undeniably true that self-assurance equips individuals with the necessary means to confront the challenges life presents, it is imperative to acknowledge that this does not guarantee an existence devoid of adversity in perpetuity. Furthermore, numerous individuals harbor a misguided belief that a crucial component in cultivating self-assurance lies solely in dedicating oneself to personal skill development and aspirations. Nevertheless, that can be perceived as a manifestation of self-centeredness. Individuals who possess genuine self-assurance inherently exhibit unwavering belief in their personal identity and abilities, both in relation to themselves and others. Such characterized behaviors enhance the likelihood of individuals to establish meaningful connections and initiate social interactions. Hence, this enables them to establish a lifestyle that is not only more harmonious but also enhances their overall well-being.

Having gained an understanding of the concept of self-confidence, let us now delve into its practical applications within real-life contexts. Self-assurance operates by facilitating the attainment of optimal levels of self-worth, thus enabling one to cultivate a sense of certainty and belief in oneself. When an individual possesses a sense of self-assurance regarding their competence to achieve objectives, it follows that they will experience heightened levels of success. Once they have achieved this success, they will acquire the necessary self-assurance to sustain their motivation towards accomplishing an even greater array of objectives. While substantial disparities can be observed between self-esteem and self-confidence, these two qualities synergistically collaborate to facilitate the development of a well-balanced self-perception in individuals.

Let us now delve into the contrasts between self-esteem and self-confidence. As it is commonly understood, self-esteem denotes an individual's perception of themselves and the extent of their self-affection. One's self-esteem is cultivated through the various encounters and circumstances encountered in their life, ultimately influencing the lens through which they perceive and evaluate themselves on a daily basis. Self-assurance pertains to the perception and emotional state that an individual holds regarding their capabilities, and this attribute demonstrates variability contingent upon the context at hand. For instance, an individual may possess robust self-esteem, yet they might experience a deficiency in self-assurance regarding their interpersonal abilities. When an individual possesses a genuine affection for themselves, their sense of self-worth is bolstered, fostering enhanced self-assurance and empowering them to embark upon novel endeavors. As an individual gains confidence in various aspects of their life, their overall self-esteem will gradually elevate. Self-assurance and self-assuredness are in symbiotic unity.

Hence, when an individual enhances their self-esteem, they simultaneously elevate their self-confidence.

Allow us to delve into the parallels that exist between the concepts of self-esteem and self-confidence. The primary resemblance they possess is the capacity for self-love. Individuals who were raised in an environment characterized by a lack of appreciation from others frequently encounter difficulties in this regard, as their upbringing lacked the necessary circumstances for cultivating self-regard. If an individual fails to perceive their worth during their formative years, it will lead to a decline in their sense of self-esteem. Should they possess inadequate faith in their own capabilities or harbor doubts about their own worth, it is likely that they will experience a deficiency in self-assurance. In a manner akin to how cultivating a positive sense of self-worth fosters an individual's self-assurance, a deficiency in self-esteem frequently results in a corresponding dearth of self-confidence.

In conclusion of this chapter, it can be asserted that self-esteem is cultivated through the myriad experiences an individual undergoes over the course of their lifetime. Self-assurance is the faculty by which an individual is capable of recognizing the inherent worth in their own abilities. The synthesis of these two concepts establishes a significant alliance within an individual, exerting substantial influence over their self-perception, their proactiveness, and their overall level of self-assurance. Kindly review the subsequent guidelines as a means to initiate the enhancement of your self-esteem and self-assurance.

- Make an effort to recall the positive attributes that are frequently acknowledged by others. Despite your personal doubts about their veracity, simply remind yourself of those beliefs. This represents the initial action towards progress.

- Endeavor to silence the pessimistic inner dialogue within your own thoughts. Endeavor to consider alternative approaches that can be employed to counterbalance or challenge those assertions.

- In the event that you find yourself harboring pessimistic thoughts about your own worth, take a moment to reflect on whether or not you would express such sentiments towards someone dear to you. If that is not the case, make an effort to refrain from harboring those thoughts.

• Compile a record of your areas of proficiency. Attempt to envision the responses you would articulate to yourself amidst a professional job interview.

Why Do Goals Fail To Yield Results For The Majority Of Individuals?

The failure of goal setting can be attributed to the lack of adherence to the necessary steps involved in establishing clear and focused goals that provide a roadmap for success. Presented below are the five underlying reasons behind the failures of most goals, along with actionable measures you can adopt to navigate these pitfalls and formulate potent goals that pave the way towards the wealth, success, happiness, and prosperity you aspire to achieve.

1. Individuals often establish exceedingly generic objectives that fail to generate a clear vision of what they strive to achieve. Objectives such as "acquire a new residence," "enhance my financial gains," and "accumulate funds for leisure travel" lack the capacity to

motivate action and fail to provide a precise aim to attain.

If you appeal to acquire a new domicile, it is advisable to establish a precise objective outlining the nature of the desired residence, its geographical region, financialery fee, aesthetic qualities, dimensions, and included amenities. Develop a concise and articulate vision of your desired outcome and articulate your objective in a written format. Please ascertain your objectives and provide precise details. The aforementioned approach is pivotal in circumventing the error of employing generic objectives.

Please strive to provide the utmost level of detail. Develop a distinct and lucid vision regarding your intended objectives. Regardless of what it may be, it is imperative to be precise and specific when establishing the objective. If your objective is to enhance the profitability of your business, ascertain the precise magnitude of increase in production you desire.

Select a specific monetary value or a percentage increment that you are resolute to achieve. If you are contemplating a holiday and aim to allocate funds for this purpose, it is advised to ascertain a specific budget, select a desired destination, and decide upon the desired activities.

Regardless of the objective, increasing the level of specificity significantly enhances one's prospects of attaining it. Why? By establishing precise and unambiguous parameters for your desired outcomes, you can ensure a firm integration of these objectives within your subconscious cognition.

Embedding your goals within your subconscious mind is a crucial element of attaining success. Once a clear vision of the goal has been established and deeply embedded in one's subconscious, it will be observed that the actions undertaken are inclined to steer towards the achievement of said goal.

2. The inability to quantify outcomes - if the objective you establish does not afford you the means to assess your progress, how will you ascertain your proximity to achievement? Having specific objectives will facilitate the measurement of progress.

Generic objectives that lack measurability are destined for failure. Conducting periodic assessments of your progress enables you to implement necessary modifications and remain on course. By rendering your objectives quantifiable, they will exert a greater impact.

3. Establishing unattainable objectives - if the goals you establish are so ambitious that they cannot be achieved within a reasonable timeframe, you will become disheartened and relinquish. Set ambitious objectives, ensuring they are within reach.

It is highly beneficial to set objectives that foster personal growth, learning, and provide substantial challenges, ultimately prompting individuals to achieve them. Nevertheless, it would be unwise to jeopardize your chances of success by harboring unrealistic expectations. Robust objectives encompass a combination of attainability and realism.

4. Establishing goals that lack relevance - ensure that the goals you set align with your long-term career and life plans, as well as your mission. Frequently, individuals often establish objectives

that may seem appealing at the moment or align with someone else's plans rather than your own.

Ensure that the objectives you set align with the desired outcome you aim to achieve; otherwise, there is little rationale in pursuing them. Do not squander your time in the pursuit of inconsequential objectives.

5. Failing to establish a designated timeframe for attainment - when goals are not bounded by time constraints, it becomes effortless to excuse oneself and refrain from taking action. Establishing a designated time frame for achieving the goal instills a sense of responsibility for taking appropriate action. It additionally permits the individual to fine-tune their actions and implement corrections throughout the process.

Should you establish an objective of accumulating sufficient funds for an envisioned vacation in June, two years henceforth, you can consistently monitor your advancements and make necessary modifications accordingly. If you failed to establish a specific timeframe and chose to wait until you were fully prepared, you might encounter unforeseen financial constraints that necessitate a deferral of your aspirations. That would be regrettable.

Place Confidence In Your Own Emotions

It is imperative to cultivate self-esteem by learning how to attentively acknowledge and rely on one's own emotions rather than instinctively reacting to the judgments of others.

A robust sense of self-worth fosters the traits of assurance, dependability, and facilitates positive social interactions. Irrespective of the circumstances, if you lack the necessary proficiency, the act of providing assistance could be considered rare. On the contrary, you may often experience a sense of being uncultured or ineffectual.

Insufficient self-regard may be a concern for certain individuals. Should an individual possess a lack of self-liking, it would subsequently impede their ability to place trust or express approval towards their own emotions or experiences. This will significantly complicate all of her connections and associations with others, while simultaneously exerting a negative impact on her overall mental well-being and daily functioning.

This matter holds significant importance. Self-confidence can have a substantial impact on various facets including personal aspirations, goals, and interpersonal relationships.

When grappling with low self-esteem, you may exacerbate the risks associated with your choices. Various matters can be reinstated without resolution, often allowed to fester and eventually explode. Insufficient self-regard may lead to inadequate self-validation or even disregard for one's own emotions. Engaging with individuals necessitates the ability to firmly hold one's own perspective regarding others and situations. Due to a diminished sense of self-worth, you may find it challenging to express your thoughts or emotions except through moments of anger.

Inadequate self-esteem can pose difficulties in efficiently achieving personal goals. If an individual lacks the conviction that she possesses the entitlement to obtain or accomplish something, how may she genuinely succeed in doing so? One instance would be encountering challenges in establishing and cultivating relationships due to the constraint imposed by your diminished self-evaluation.

In a similar vein, diminished self-confidence can engender a sense of distrust towards others. It is possible that you may perceive a sense of obligation towards another individual, or fear that they will not demonstrate genuine concern for you upon getting to know you better. In order to maintain their presence in your life, it may be advisable to refrain from discussing sensitive matters until they accumulate and lead to feelings of resentment, thus causing a strain on your relationships with friends and family.

One of the benefits of having self-esteem is that it empowers individuals to establish goals and strive towards their achievement. You may not perceive yourself as deserving of concepts such as connections, satisfaction, and achievement. Self-esteem is the underlying factor that bestows upon you a sense of worth and significance.

Frequently, we are often instructed to "Place absolute faith in your intuition," however, what does this phrase signify and, more importantly, how can one go about implementing it?

Intuition, also known as a gut feeling, refers to an immediate, innate understanding of something without the need for extensive contemplation or analysis; it is a matter of sheer knowing without requiring further deliberation or alternative viewpoints. Your instinct manifests as an innate proclivity within your being that you personally perceive. Given the proximity of the inclination to your personal experience, no one else possesses the capability to inform you of the alignment between your actions and your intuitive instinct. The decision lies solely in your hands. Due to this, placing faith in your instinct is essentially a conclusive manifestation of self-reliance.

By tapping into your intuition, you can effectively avoid unfavorable relationships and situations. On a daily basis, a multitude of individuals will formulate opinions on what is in your best interest, comprising of well-intentioned perspectives as well as those driven by misguided, potentially harmful, or self-centered motives. Determining an individual's social class can sometimes pose challenges, yet if one disregards external presumptions and instead relies on one's own intuition, it will aptly guide towards what truly suits them.

The path to trusting one's intuition is more challenging than the idiom implies, particularly when certain ingrained behaviors and circumstances consistently and inadvertently push us in an opposing direction. Fortunately, our instinct is deeply ingrained, such that even if we have been disconnected from it throughout our lifetime, it remains embedded within us, eagerly awaiting our invocation of its wisdom.

Your intuition bears a striking resemblance to your personal guiding star, yet there are multiple obstacles that act as veils, diminishing its luminosity. When you are mindful of them, you will better catch yourself when you are going off course for the misguided reasons so you would then be able to find a way to realign with your instinct. These are the guilty parties:

Excessive contemplation: Given that instinct is defined as the ability to grasp something intuitively, without the necessity of deliberate cognition, overthinking proves to be a significant impediment. Engaging in thorough deliberation and carefully considering various scenarios and outcomes can often distance oneself from their innate intuition, especially when one is prone to excessive contemplation in an attempt to justify or authenticate a particular decision. In such instances, your viewpoint does not flow openly or organically, but rather adheres to a highly specific strategy aimed at contriving evidence in support of a predetermined conclusion. In various circumstances, the proliferation of possibilities and thoughts generated by excessive rumination can become overwhelming and perplexing, ultimately trapping you in a bewildering cycle with no apparent guidance. This particular state is commonly referred to as analysis paralysis. Irrespective of adhering to the appropriate protocol, excessive analysis leads you to a comparable state - detached from your innate intuition.

Expectations: Expectations often come into play when one is overanalyzing or during instances of apparent engagement. For example, if you have concerns about whether or not [someone else] will approve of me if I take this action. In these instances, you are evaluating your behavior based on the standards, preferences, and expectations set by someone else, instead of introspecting and allowing your own ideas and desires to guide your actions. This would cause you to ask a different question such as, "What impact will this have on my self-esteem?" Because "shoulds" divert the focus away from oneself, they create a disconnect from your intuition.

Prejudices and Unconscious Bias: Despite preferences and unconscious inclinations being somewhat contradictory to excessive rumination, they significantly influence one's instinct. Instead of engaging in excessive contemplation and extensive analysis, prejudices and unconscious bias operate on hasty judgments made by the brain, which are instinctively based on past experiences, generalizations, and background rather than on rationality or firsthand knowledge. Hence, both of these wrongdoers fail to allow room for you to exploit the experiential concept of intuition.

The needs, requirements, assessment, and guidance of acquaintances, relatives, or authoritative individuals: Oftentimes, it is these close associates or authoritative figures, such as parents, partners, educators, or mentors, who possess the greatest ability to obscure or hinder your instinctual judgment, but whose affection or approbation you strive to obtain.

When experiencing a profound longing for something: When faced with an intense hunger for something, be it love, recognition, children, social status, or any other desire, the overwhelming compulsion to satisfy that immense need may cause you to disregard or disregard any cautionary signs along the way. Maintaining unwavering focus on fulfilling a righteous objective significantly diminishes the opportunity to acknowledge or pursue one's instinct, particularly when that innate perception contradicts an individual or entity closely aligned with said objective.

Childhood trauma: Among the myriad culprits, one of the most profound contributors is the experience of mistreatment and violence during early years. Why? From an early age, therapeutic interventions can have a long-lasting impact on an individual that persists well into their adult years. The experience of being subjected to physical, emotional, or potentially sexual abuse during one's formative years can instill self-doubt in children and lead them to blame themselves. Given that trusting your intuition is essentially akin to comprehension, harnessing this inherent gut instinct can pose a challenge.

When one leads a sheltered existence and constantly rushes, whether in a physical or mental sense, important details are overlooked. Slackening necessitates that you duly comprehend and integrate the information you receive, both mentally and physically. In order to accomplish this, one must engage in a thorough and systematic process of tidying both mentally and physically. In actuality, it can be perceived as extending the deadline in order to alleviate the urgency surrounding a decision. It could also imply distancing oneself from a situation in order to gain greater clarity, such as taking a break before making a career transition or spending time apart from one's partner to assess compatibility.

Deliberately creating room for your intuition to become engaged is what is implied by the term 'slackening'. The deliberate pace facilitates a shift in your perspective, allowing for the accumulation of various distractions, thereby enabling you to ascertain and experience what truly holds significance. Examine introspection, yogic exercises, deliberate respiration techniques, and varied methodologies that redirect your attention away from racing thoughts towards a profound state of tranquility and concentrated mindfulness within yourself.

Intuition is inherently linked to the bodily sensations, therefore, it is imperative to develop the ability to perceive one's inner bodily experiences, such as emotions, as it greatly facilitates the strengthening of intuition. Although we interchangeably use the terms "feelings" and "sensations" to describe instinct, it is important to recognize a subtle distinction. Primarily, our primary focus lies in understanding how your body physically responds to a feeling rather than simply labeling the emotion, such as bitterness, anger, or confusion, and stopping at that. For instance, we are particularly interested in examining the physical manifestations of anger, which may include tightness, soreness, heat, and tingling sensations. A remarkable approach for practicing would be to recollect the emotional state during an experience, such as anger, and subsequently discern the bodily sensations correlated with that emotion. For instance, one might perceive that their jaw tightens and their shoulders elevate and become tense. Engaging in this practice helps you to clear your mind, as failing to do so leaves room for thoughts to overpower you, and instead directs your focus towards your body, where your intuition resides.

Begin practising as a novice observer, observing with curiosity the unfolding of changes in your bodily reactions, improvements, and sensations. Conducted evaluations of reflections through guided body assessments prove to be especially advantageous in refining this skill. So are exercises in which one deduces a specific recollection and subsequently identifies and experiences the sensations it incites within oneself. When engaging in these activities, take into account the evaluation of your breathing, muscular state, and pulse, in order to discern the bodily response and the corresponding insights it may provide. The contained information is crucial for devising activities that hold significance and relevance to you.

Pose the question to yourself, "What are my genuine needs in this situation?" What holds paramount importance for me? This is one of those instances where the focus must solely be on your individuality, thus granting yourself the complete freedom to act accordingly. In the event that you find your attention shifting towards other individuals and their needs, make a conscious effort to redirect your focus towards understanding and prioritizing your own desires and requirements. This is where your intuition lies, and by attending to these necessities, you pave a clear and effective path towards it. In order to eliminate any ambiguity regarding your intuition, it would be beneficial to first examine the aforementioned roster of culprits to identify the external factors that are influencing you. By acknowledging these factors, you can subsequently disregard them for the time being. Your intuition is an integral facet of your highest intellectual capacity, thus it is imperative to focus squarely on your own judgement.

The sensation of instinct bears resemblance to the ebb and flow of a sea tide, guiding you towards a life of fulfillment. Once the discovery is made, regardless of any obstacles encountered, one must embark upon a vessel and commence a voyage in order to ascertain its true value. Once you have responded to the query "What do I require at present?", proceed to devise a course of action to fulfill your needs. Although it may be the smallest progress, its magnitude is insignificant in this context. Initial progress can prove beneficial in establishing a foundation of trust with your intuitive faculties, as they may resurface for the first time following a period of isolation caused by a distressing relationship. What is of significance is that you are heeding your innate intuition.

It is important to bear in mind that trusting one's instincts is an ongoing process that often necessitates revisiting these methods, especially when circumstances evolve and life continues to progress. Consider your intuition as a strength to strengthen. Through deliberate and ongoing practice, it will evolve into a more prominent and proficient entity, effectively fulfilling its purpose of home management for your personal use.

You Are What You Eat

I often experience a sense of melancholy, typically on Mondays and Tuesdays, as I typically bear the consequences of Saturday night. Furthermore, my employment within the public sector failed to instill a sense of fulfillment and vitality in me. Typically, on Tuesday evenings, I would engage in athletics, involving rigorous interval training sessions that encompassed sprints ranging from 100 to 400 meters, causing significant physical exertion. This was hard work but afterwards, I would feel great. All of a sudden, vitality surged within me once again.

During a different period in my life, I was enduring a challenging situation. I encountered considerable challenges in the realm of romantic relationships and experienced some degree of stress in my professional pursuits. During my commute home, I would frequently make a brief detour to the nearby store to acquire essential food items, occasionally indulging in the purchase of vegan chocolate treats as well. This transient gratification, nonetheless, instilled a sense of unease and exacerbated my state afterwards. The influx of detrimental thoughts would resurface within my mind, subsequently inducing renewed distress.

I observed this trend to a certain extent and subsequently decided to consume nutritious whole foods exclusively during weekdays, resume my fasting routine, and return to my regular workout regimen. Merely addressing this aspect did not alleviate my difficulties; however, I began to experience an improvement in my well-being as I prioritized self-care once more.

When contemplating the concepts of nutrition and exercise, our focus commonly shifts to our physical aesthetics - With the presumption that adhering to a healthy diet and engaging in regular physical activity will enhance our overall physique, while neglecting these practices will result in a less favorable state of physical wellness. This statement holds true based on my individual experiences and personal growth journey; however, it is important to acknowledge that the impacts of nutrition and exercise extend far beyond what we currently comprehend.

A prominent literary work that I will once again invoke, just as I did in my preceding publication, is the renowned piece of literature and accompanying educational program titled 'Unstoppable', authored by Ben Angel. A literary work that effectively delves into the intricate connections between diet, physical activity, and their profound impacts on one's physical well-being, psychological state, and emotional equilibrium.

I strongly endorse this course, specifically.

What relevance does this hold in relation to one's self-esteem? Based on the narrative's illustrations and my earlier remarks, it can be deduced that by consuming unhealthy food, one implies a self-perception aligned with such choices. By adopting a mindful approach to self-care, individuals can experience heightened vitality, improved cognitive acuity, and an enhanced sense of self-contentment.

It is crucial to acknowledge that each individual possesses distinct sensitivities, preferences, and dietary requirements. It is crucial to ascertain what aligns with your needs and preferences, in order to cultivate a sense of well-being.

Regarding physical activity, you may be aware that engaging in exercise stimulates the production of endorphins, which are chemicals that induce a sense of pleasure and well-being in the body. Physical activity does not necessarily require engaging in a daily marathon or spending two hours each day, but rather can be achieved through twenty to thirty minutes of exercise. Ideally, an activity that will induce perspiration. You are affirming to your body and mind that you possess inherent value. One must prioritize self-care as it is an essential act of self-love.

A highly effective method for enhancing one's self-awareness regarding nutrition and exercise involves the practice of diligently maintaining a journal, which leads me to address your subsequent course of action...

Action:

At the conclusion of each day, retrieve your journal and generate two enumerations. One list pertains to "experiences that brought me joy today and actions that I should engage in more frequently." The other list addresses "experiences that did not elicit favorable feelings, accompanied by strategies to eliminate them from my life."

By deliberately selecting which exercise and nutrition pursuits elicit positive sensations, one will gradually differentiate between beneficial and detrimental habits. Acquiring knowledge about these factors and discerning appropriate measures can lead to an enhanced sense of well-being, thereby fostering a stronger sense of personal worth.

The Influence Of Optimistic Thought Patterns

Stage Three - Harnessing the Potential of Optimistic Thought

There is no superior method to swiftly enhance one's self-esteem than the approach being emphasized here. Step 3 entails the practice of maintaining a mindset focused on optimism and constructive thoughts. Positive thinking encompasses one's cognitive and affective disposition to concentrate on constructive aspects and to have a proactive anticipation of favorable outcomes in one's life. This anticipation has the ability to elevate an individual from a state of diminished self-confidence to a state of embracing oneself.

The potency of embracing optimistic thoughts can pave the way for achieving robust physical well-being, contentment, and triumphant accomplishments in one's journey through life. The efficacy of maintaining an optimistic mindset culminates in fostering an inherent set of beliefs, enabling individuals to surmount adversities, setbacks, and challenges.

In order for you to achieve success and enhance your self-esteem, adopting a mindset of optimism and constructive thought patterns is imperative, transcending mere verbal expressions. It is imperative for it to transform into a state of existence rather than simply a state of cognition. Let us examine the components of this matter.

• The Influence of Thought and Ideas

Many individuals frequently find it difficult to embrace the notion that the power of thoughts and ideas can effectively bring about tangible outcomes within the material world. The notion that one can manifest their thoughts into reality is, to a certain extent, "inconceivable". Nevertheless, this statement holds true and requires only a limited number of examples to be convincing.

Let us examine two individuals striving for a common objective. One individual harbors the conviction that they will attain it, while the other individual maintains the belief that they will be unsuccessful in obtaining it. What do think happens? What if two groups were to strive for the same triumph? The collective belief of the entire team is that they will emerge victorious. The opposing team comprises individuals with varying opinions, as some are confident in their chances of winning, while others express doubt. Additionally, there are those who possess the necessary skills to win yet harbor apprehension about their prospects.

What are your thoughts regarding the potential outcome? The core inquiry resides in what our collective experience indicates is likely to unfold.

In initial circumstances, individuals who possess unwavering faith in their ability to achieve a target are likely to succeed, while those lacking self-confidence will invariably fall short of the same goal. The team that possesses a collective belief in their impending victory will ultimately emerge as the triumphant party. Additionally, a valuable lesson can be gleaned from the collective confidence exhibited by the team, firmly convinced of their impending victory and ultimately achieving it. Positive thinking is contagious. Furthermore, there is a valuable lesson to be gleaned from the team that did not emerge victorious - namely, the contagious nature of pessimistic thoughts.

The influence of our surrounding individuals on us is significant, regardless of whether it is overt, subliminal, or intuitive. Their body language, their words, their feelings and their thoughts affect us on an instinctive and subconscious level.

Pessimistic thought patterns give rise to adverse emotions and conduct. Similarly, just as cultivating a positive mindset stimulates the emergence of constructive emotions and conduct. Conversely, individuals seek our presence, extend their assistance, and favorable circumstances manifest themselves as a result. It is essential that we maintain a heightened level of awareness regarding any detrimental emotions that arise within our consciousness and promptly address them.

Develop the ability to effectively substitute your negative thoughts with constructive ones by means of self-guided learning. Engage in this practice whenever a negative thought arises in your mind. Be persistent. It will eventually work. You are nurturing and cultivating your mental faculties, just as individuals have perpetually engaged in throughout history. Whether you are aware of it or not, you are actively conditioning your mind to adopt a positive outlook. Let us explore alternative methods of cultivating your cognitive abilities.

- Affirmations by Louise Hay

Louise Hay is an individual residing in the United States who found herself diagnosed with a terminal illness, however, she possessed a resolute determination to alter this prevailing reality. Medical professionals stated that there were no viable options, yet Louise held unwavering faith in the power of the mind to transcend physical limitations. Put differently, it can be asserted that mental processes have the ability to manifest tangible existence. Louise applied her personal beliefs, crafting a unique methodology and set of affirmations, initially for the purpose of preserving her own life. Subsequently, she extended her efforts to assist others in rescuing and enhancing their own lives.

The utilization of affirmations serves as the pivotal factor in Hay's ability to persevere and in elevating one's self-worth. Her inaugural of numerous literary works stands as her renowned masterpiece, titled You Can Heal Your Life. She is an innovator in the discipline of affirmations, serving as evidence that adopting a positive mindset can yield tangible and psychological transformations. Utilizing positive assertions can enhance your self-confidence IMMEDIATELY. It will require unwavering commitment and unwavering perseverance from you, but it will yield the desired outcome.

Affirmations refer to constructive thoughts that are regularly voiced aloud, aiming to foster optimism within oneself. Affirmations are phrases that encapsulate positive and empowering thoughts, exemplified by the renowned affirmation coined by Louise Hay: 'With each passing day, I am progressing and growing in an increasingly remarkable manner.' Consistently engaging with the material found in her books along with diligently utilizing her tapes provides an assured path towards rapidly enhancing one's self-esteem.

- A Formal Inquiry into Miraculous Phenomena • A Study on the

Phenomenon of Miracles • An Investigative Examination of Miraculous Occurrences • An Academic Exploration of Miraculous Events • An Analytical Study on the Concept of Miracles

A Course in Miracles can be regarded as a literary work authored and revised by Helen Schuman, and transcribed and edited by William Thetford. Its fundamental notion closely aligns with the concepts previously deliberated upon in this chapter. The "Workbook" holds primary significance as it provides a daily lesson for each day of the year. The purpose of these lessons is to facilitate a transformation in one's mindset, shifting from a paradigm of "condemnation driven by fear" to one of "forgiveness driven by love."

Once again, the authors assert that a change in one's cognitive perspective is instrumental in precipitating subsequent modifications in behavior and emotions, not only for the individual who undergoes the cognitive shift but also for those in their immediate vicinity. The teachings highlight our collective unity with everything, as well as the imperative of cultivating self-forgiveness and extending forgiveness to others. The workbook requests that you place trust in its recommendations for daily actions, with the eventual outcome being the manifestation of the desired reality and personal transformation.

It is possible that you may encounter considerable difficulty in engaging with A Course in Miracles. The concept revolves around envisioning life and oneself according to one's desired circumstances, subsequently leveraging the power of thought to manifest these intentions, regardless of one's level of belief in their attainability. Should you presently observe and project your diminished self-regard, desolation, and resentment outward, you shall behold yourself and the world through that lens. Alternatively, if one acquires the ability to express love and forgiveness towards others, they will consequently perceive themselves and the world through a similar lens, resulting in an elevation of their self-esteem. Above all, it is crucial to demonstrate self-forgiveness.

• Recapitulation and Course of Action

In the preceding chapter, we have examined the notion of materializing our thoughts into tangible reality, thereby shaping the physical realm through the power of our thoughts. One cultivates their level of self-esteem through the power of their thoughts, and it is possible to acquire the skill of positive thinking. Outlined below are a number of actions that can assist you in attaining this objective.

The Benefits of a Positive Mindset in Achieving Success and Beyond

Leading a life characterized by optimism can yield multiple advantages. Initially, one may not perceive it, but there exists a remarkable disparity between this perspective and that of harboring negative thoughts, comparable to the contrast between night and day.

Engage in constructive positive self-dialogue, which involves actively addressing negative thoughts that arise. Additionally, it fosters enhanced cognitive organization and proficiency through continuous dedication and training.

Maintaining a positive outlook is no easy feat. It will require diligent practice similar to all other endeavors. Baby steps have to be taken, but after gradual practice, you'll soon get the hang of it.

The exercise of positivity leads to the accomplishment of uncomplicated tasks. It is of such inherent simplicity that it may evoke a sense of wonderment as to why one has not undertaken it at the earliest possible opportunity.

Regarding the phenomena of the cloud and its accompanying silver lining

It's true. Indeed, while it may appear that the album is characterized by repetitive elements and an overarching sense of cliché, adopting a perspective that recognizes the inherent positivity in all circumstances would prove to be considerably more beneficial. Even in adverse circumstances, there remains a positive aspect.

Challenging circumstances may be perceived as opportunities for personal growth and self-improvement.

Encountering loss can be perceived as a poignant reminder of the inherent value of the things that hold significance in one's life, prompting a deeper appreciation for the present assets that persist.

Take delight in the modest joys of existence.

All occasions have the potential to be commemorated and savored.

Did you experience a challenging day at the workplace? Regard this as a chance to arrange a gathering subsequently.

Doing chores? View it as an opportunity for introspection and contemplation, as well as a means to expend energy if your aim is weight loss.

Take heed of the intricacies of existence and perceive their potential as sources of gratification.

Examine both oneself and others through a positive lens. There exists inherent goodness within every individual; it is incumbent upon us to recognize and acknowledge it.

3. Positive Self-Talk

Engaging in affirmative self-communication is paramount to achieving personal success. If one is able to alter the internal dialogue, one possesses the capability to achieve anything.

Numerous research studies have demonstrated that the human brain is capable of undergoing significant changes even during the later stages of adulthood. This phenomenon is referred to as "neuroplasticity."

Each and every cognitive notion we generate, whether it be explicit or latent, is converted into electrical impulses that subsequently regulate the range of emotions we experience, the language we articulate, and the behaviors we exhibit.

We encode our minds through the language we use to communicate with ourselves.

It serves as the cognitive faculty of the mind.

Hence, self-dialogue also presents a chance to supplant our previous negative conditioning through the utilization of repetition.

Thus, what is the appropriate approach to accomplish this task? By what means can we employ self-dialogue to alter the incessant internal discourse taking place within our minds?

The solution is straightforward - we utilize appropriate linguistic expressions.

Employing affirmative and present-time expressions, such as "I am," "at present, I acknowledge," or "I am in the process of," underscores the ongoing transformations occurring in the current instance. In the not too remote future. As an illustration, consider the statement, "I am committed to developing my moral character," and observe how it resonates with you.

Not very inspiring, eh?

Please express the following statement: "I possess positive qualities and exhibit morally upright behavior."

How did that feel?

Significant rewiring of the brain can be achieved by regularly incorporating positive statements in the present tense into one's daily routine. Replace the antiquated and detrimental inner dialogue with a constructive alternative and diligently reinforce it during brief intervals of leisure.

A selection of self-affirming phrases that I hold dear include:

\\\"I am enough.\\\"

I am capable of accomplishing this task.

The constant presence of the divine is forever by my side.

I have emerged as the victor.

Today belongs to me.

I am worthy of the highest quality, and I consistently strive to perform at my utmost potential.

\\\"I forgive myself.\\\"

I have great affection and unconditional acceptance for myself.

I possess inherent value and deserve to receive love without any conditions or alterations to my true self.

The act of consistently reaffirming these positive affirmations not only exerts a significant beneficial impact on my own life but also extends its influence to those with whom I choose to share them. You are welcome to either adopt these suggestions or develop new ones customized to meet your specific requirements.

If you are going to create new ones yourself, make sure they are positive and in the present tense.

Become More Self-Aware

After self-awareness, comes self-management.
Self-management pertains to the capacity to exercise personal direction with mindful and conscientious consideration of one's behaviors.
Let us endeavor to reflect upon a previous occasion wherein you exhibited a logical and advantageous choice amidst the fleeting frenzy elicited by emotional impulses. Can you honestly remember? How frequently did you subsequently engage in this behavior once you became conscious of it?

As previously demonstrated, the neural activity in the brain precipitated by heightened emotional states typically occurs swiftly, outpacing the engagement of the cognitive faculties responsible for rational decision-making. This reasoning is the cause behind occurrences where individuals tend to commit irrational and occasionally foolish errors while experiencing heightened emotional states. For this very reason, young couples who are consumed by intense emotions often choose to elope or enter into hasty marriages. Due to our lack of rationality, we have engaged in conflicts that could have been prevented had we dedicated additional time to deliberate before taking action. This reason may potentially account for the loss of employment and fractured relationships among individuals.

However, once you initiate the cultivation of self-awareness, this subsequent aspect becomes considerably more manageable to adhere to. If anything, it is closely linked to one's sense of self-awareness. Upon gaining consciousness of your triggers, you will acquire the ability to more effectively evaluate circumstances and proactively strategize your response when faced with circumstances or individuals that push you to your limits.

By consciously opting to be emotionally engaged, you will subsequently develop the capacity to absorb distressing information or confront tense circumstances without it jeopardizing your rational faculties.

If an individual were to grapple with anger, achieving self-awareness would entail recognizing the stimuli that incite fury. Then, self-management follows through. Given your awareness of the factors that trigger your anger, you will commence making choices conducive to preemptively combating its full encroachment upon your psyche.

In the event of experiencing excessive trepidation, you shall gain an understanding of the underlying causes of your anxiety, subsequently embarking upon a deliberate course of action aimed at triumphing over said fear.

However, in order to proceed with this stage, it is imperative to exhibit unwavering dedication and engage in substantial contemplation. Due to our inherent inclination towards maintaining the status quo, our cognitive faculties frequently dissuade us from embracing transformative endeavors. Indeed, your mental faculties are impeding your pursuit of a more fulfilling trajectory.

Change is scary. Due to this factor, you will discover a preference for remaining in familiar surroundings. The task of consciously coordinating and maneuvering oneself within the realms of existence can be quite daunting. This will result in your subsequent discomfort with the activities that previously brought you pleasure. It entails acknowledging and accepting one's shortcomings, gaining a conscious understanding of the impact that one's previously unconscious behaviors have on their interpersonal connections and overall psychological well-being. Hence, undertaking the task of effectively controlling one's emotional reactions shall prove challenging. Additionally, one cannot deny the profound sense of fulfillment that arises from faithfully expressing one's emotions. You believe that your actions are morally justified. The surge of adrenaline experienced in that instant creates the illusion of heroic action. You possess great bravery and fearlessness, demonstrating a capacity for rationality and critical thinking, rather than being driven solely by emotions. Therefore, it is possible for individuals to develop a dependence on perpetuating this pattern of emotional turmoil. However fleeting it may be, the lasting repercussions of an emotional response to any given circumstance become apparent over time.

Once you attain a deeper awareness of your emotions, you will consequently cultivate a greater capacity for compassion towards individuals facing their own challenges, thereby fostering a genuine desire to assist them. Does embracing self-forgiveness correspond to extending forgiveness towards others? When one lacks emotional alignment, their state of being will invariably manifest itself in their interactions with others. You experience irritation towards another individual due to your own susceptibility to short-temperedness. You deride a fellow individual afflicted by apprehension due to your own personal difficulty with trepidation. All of these concerns contribute to rendering you unresponsive to treatment and incapable of engaging in social interactions.

Enhanced emotional management facilitates improved interpersonal connections. Instead of reducing them to their emotional state of being, you perceive their struggle, as it is an experience that you share, having grappled with it as well, and therefore, can empathize with. You subsequently emanate a captivating presence by comprehending the other individual's emotional state and facilitating the initiation of their journey towards enhanced emotional management.

Self-confidence vs self esteem
In actuality, despite occasional interchangeability, it should be noted

that self-confidence and self-esteem possess distinct implications.

Self-esteem: what is it?

Self-esteem is intricately connected to self-worth, which pertains to the level of significance you attribute to your own being. To evaluate your self-esteem, inquire within yourself: to what extent do I feel at ease embracing my true self? To what degree do I perceive my worthiness of experiencing happiness and achieving success? Providing forthright responses to these and comparable inquiries will empower you to ascertain the worth you attribute to oneself.

An additional component of self-worth is the perception of one's sense of inclusion, namely the degree to which one experiences acceptance and admiration from others. The "others" refer to individuals who hold significant importance in your life and whose opinions carry weight, such as your family members or colleagues.

Self-esteem, henceforth, is defined as an individual's perception of their own worth, encompassing their physical appearance, cognitive processes, and sense of recognition. The presence of that inherent quality of "otherness" primarily arises from the fact that your sense of self-worth is constructed from the array of experiences and interpersonal connections you have encountered throughout your life. Every individual you have encountered has had an impact on either augmenting or diminishing your perception of self.

Understanding the concept of self-confidence: what does it entail?

In contrast, self-assurance entails the firm belief in one's own abilities and personal potential.

Upon encountering individuals uttering the phrases, "I possess confidence in regards to abc, however..." and "I am utterly assured of my ability to...", what thoughts are evoked within you? These two scenarios suggest that confidence exists on a spectrum. Allow us to acquire further insights pertaining to these levels.

Confidence Levels

The degree of self-assurance you maintain is not consistent across all days and all circumstances. Our confidence levels can fluctuate, and there are days when our assurance in our abilities is greater than on others. These fluctuations can occasionally be attributed to the extant conditions, such as your proficiency level in a given task, familiarity with a particular role or individuals involved, the seriousness of the situation (as in facing a job interview panel as opposed to learning to prepare a new dish), and your emotional resilience, to provide a few examples.

The degree of self-assurance typically becomes evident to both the individual as the subject of the role and to observers. This is attributable to the inferences that can be drawn from your non-verbal cues and mannerisms. For instance, one's confidence is influenced by subtleties such as graceful movements, vibrant vocal intonations, strong and arid handshakes, direct eye contact, or stooped posture, regardless of one's conscious awareness of these factors.

Does this imply that one has the potential to possess an insufficient or excessive amount of confidence, or perhaps reaching the extremes, considering that confidence exhibits varying degrees?
Is it feasible to possess an excessive amount of self-assurance?
An excessive degree of self-assurance often manifests as an air of arrogance, wherein one perceives or conducts themselves as superior to others. The pronounced disposition towards entitlement and exaggerated emphasis on personal achievements vis-à-vis others can engender aggressive conduct. In order to address this, it is advisable to bear in mind that regardless of one's accomplishments or capabilities, imperfection is inherent and, like any individual, one possesses a blend of virtues, limitations, and shortcomings.
Is it conceivable to possess an inadequate amount of self-assurance?

Indeed, the response to this query is an unequivocal affirmation. Numerous individuals are burdened by a dearth of assurance or diminished self-assurance.

To facilitate the differentiation between a reasonable level of self-assurance and diminished self-assurance, presented below are several frequently observed behavioral indicators. Which thoughts and behaviors are discernible within oneself and among others? Gaining insight into the patterns of behavior associated with your self-assurance can aid in assessing the state of your confidence, gauging its well-being.

Upon examining these few couplings, it is evident that possessing self-assurance is considerably more appealing, whereas lacking self-assurance implies a sense of negativity, insufficiency, and a condition that can only prove to be detrimental.

One's self-perception and inner dialogue possess the potential to either uplift or undermine their overall well-being and success. In a general sense, self-assurance plays a pivotal role in shaping the trajectory of our lives. It is the distinguishing factor between soaring high with the grace of an eagle or remaining grounded, confined to mundane endeavors akin to a chicken scratching the dirt. Self-assurance, too, serves as a vital antecedent to the choices we make regarding our career paths, life partners, and interpersonal relationships, amongst other facets of life.

Upon careful observation, one cannot overlook the profound impact of low self-confidence, ranging from severe outcomes such as suicide, self-mutilation, eating disorders, and substance abuse, to relatively milder manifestations like persistent indecisiveness.

What are the potential advantages that come with possessing a strong sense of self-assurance? Allow me to elucidate a few of the manners in which you can derive advantages from possessing self-assurance.

The benefits that accompany possessing self-assurance

The majority of individuals can affirm that possessing confidence greatly enhances the likelihood of achieving success and fulfillment in various aspects of life. Presented herein are several methods by which cultivating confidence can bestow happiness upon one's existence.

#Enhances Performance

Insufficient self-assurance can significantly hinder the achievement of your optimal performance. Consider an instance in which the apprehension of failure deterred you from assuming a novel obligation. Now envision a coworker who willingly offered their services with unwavering confidence, firmly believing that any gaps in their knowledge can be readily filled through learning or assistance from others. It is highly likely that your colleague performed exceptionally well, which led to their receiving a salary increase or being assigned more significant and demanding tasks to enhance their prominence within the organization.

What about you? What did you gain? Opacity; persistently ensnared in an employment position devoid of professional advancement or intellectual development, despite harboring the conviction of possessing superior capabilities compared to one's peer. Your inadequacy in self-assurance prevented you from surmounting challenges and effectively harnessing your existing abilities to achieve success.

Increased Levels of Happiness

Self-confident people are a happy lot. You experience a reduced level of concerns and anxieties, you do not feel obligated to conform to others' expectations, you assertively seek and obtain your necessities without compromising, and you are less inclined to engage in detrimental rivalries or be daunted by someone else's achievements.

Having a sufficient amount of self-assurance enables individuals to approach life situations with vigor and resolve, leading to the cultivation of meaningful connections, the production of high-caliber work, and a sense of interconnectedness with one's environment. Furthermore, the expression of confidence can significantly influence the behavior of others, fostering their inclination to support your leadership, endorse your choices, seek affiliation with you, and regard you as an exemplar. Ultimately, this solidifies your sense of significance and purpose in society.

#Better Health

"When one possesses a sound sense of self-assurance and self-worth, they are more adequately prepared to:

*Mitigate the influence of negative peers - as you do not succumb to societal pressures for acceptance or conformity, you demonstrate a reduced likelihood to engage in misconduct such as reckless sexual behavior, involvement in criminal gangs, and substance abuse. Consequently, you effectively evade the various health hazards linked to such behaviors.

Embrace a nutritious diet – a deficiency in self-acceptance or self-love can diminish one's self-esteem and confidence, consequently prompting the utilization of food as a means of emotional solace. This results in the development of disorders such as binge eating and bulimia, which have deleterious effects on your health.

Enhance your mental well-being - With increased self-assurance, you perceive mistakes as a typical outcome of existence, enabling personal growth and resilience. One embraces the perspective that occasional errors are permissible, acknowledging one's inherent humanity, and subsequently proceeds forward. Nevertheless, individuals who possess an absence of self-assurance are prone to magnify minor issues into major ones. You engage in self-criticism, perceive oneself as being scrutinized and inadequately judged by others, and occasionally resort to drastic measures to conceal one's mistakes. Typically, individuals tend to enter a state of heightened stress, resulting in the manifestation of symptoms such as anxiety attacks, depressive episodes, irrational apprehensions, specific phobias, and a tendency to isolate oneself from supportive and nurturing social connections.

Emotional Stability

Self-assurance fosters a profound sense of inner equilibrium derived from possessing comprehensive understanding, embracing, and valuing oneself. You possess the ability to establish objectives, successfully attain them, and steadfastly adhere to ethical guidelines that contribute positively to your well-being. In doing so, you prevent yourself from descending into the treacherous realm of emotional vulnerability driven by the desire for validation and acceptance. You desist from actively pursuing validation and seeking attention from others. Cease basing your self-worth on the opinions or perceptions of others, and refrain from sacrificing your own needs in order to appease their fleeting desires. You prioritize your own needs, demonstrating a commendable level of self-care and self-acceptance.

Less Self-sabotage

At times, we can be our own most formidable adversaries, burdened by an extensive mental register (possibly even documented) of obligations, convictions, and principles we feel compelled to abide by, along with aspirations we strive to achieve. The primary aspect that raises my apprehension regarding these beliefs, values, and expectations pertains to their practicality and logicality in terms of achievability.

In our pursuit of achievement, as defined within the context of our respective social collectives encompassing familial, occupational, spiritual, cultural, or any alternative affiliations, we inadvertently establish a restrictive system of societal expectations. For instance, "I ought to attain the position of branch manager before a specific age...I ought to maintain a particular weight..." We endeavor to abide by this roster of ideals, and when we fail to meet them, as is frequently the case, our self-assurance significantly diminishes.

Nevertheless, when one possesses self-assurance, they eschew this pursuit of perfection and instead adhere to feasible benchmarks that are predominantly predicated on their aptitude and perspective on life. You endeavor to improve upon yourself, focusing neither on surpassing others nor emulating them.

#Enjoy Happier Relationships

One's state of happiness is enhanced when they possess confidence or a sense of self-assurance. Consequently, individuals who exhibit such positive qualities naturally draw in other individuals who are both happy and confident. Due to your diminished level of dependence (reduced need for reassurance, acceptance, affirmation), you exhibit a higher degree of compatibility, companionship, and cohabitation. You do not exhibit excessive sensitivity and possess a greater ability to approach matters from a rational standpoint, resulting in a diminished occurrence of exaggerated responses, disputes, and conflicts.

An individual who possesses self-assurance tends to exhibit a propensity for generosity within interpersonal dynamics. In this manner, interacting with you proves to be advantageous to others, as you possess the ability to genuinely reciprocate emotions, exhibit helpfulness and generosity beyond the norm, as well as showcase remarkable reliability and resourcefulness. There is an increased likelihood that individuals will desire your company. An individual's possession of self-assurance is an exceedingly captivating attribute.

#Social Ease

Individuals who possess a strong sense of self-assurance exhibit charming attributes that instill a sense of comfort in others and facilitate seamless interactions, even in unfamiliar social settings. These attributes comprise the capacity to actively listen, refrain from interrupting discourse, maintain appropriate levels of eye contact, possess the skill of understanding when and what to communicate, offer sincere commendations, avoid excessive criticism, and never engage in acts of diminishing others.

Why? This occurs due to the fact that when one possesses confidence, their attention is not solely fixated on themselves, but rather directed towards others. When an individual receives your focused attention, they experience a sense of significance, worth, captivation, and joy. Individuals who possess intrinsic confidence additionally display a sanguine outlook and zealous attitude towards forthcoming prospects. This is evident in their demeanor, gait, speech, and manner of self-expression. They emit a robust and captivating positive aura, which has a contagious effect and is appealing to others.

Upon recognizing the numerous advantages associated with confidence, as well as the hindrances that can arise from a lack thereof in accomplishing one's objectives, the subsequent undertaking entails acquiring the knowledge and skills necessary to effectively cultivate unparalleled levels of self-assurance. I will impart this knowledge to you through the provision of 20 effective strategies that have the potential to profoundly alter your life indefinitely. Prior to delving into this topic, it is essential that we first examine the factors that led to the deterioration of our once thriving self-assurance.

Exercise Careful Consideration Prior to Uttering Words
Exercise caution and reflection before expressing oneself, or refrain from speaking altogether. This is a matter that you will need to resolve independently. Certain individuals require a greater emphasis on a particular area, while others would benefit from concentrating on the alternative aspect. The majority of individuals have the capacity to cultivate equilibrium within their lives. What is the specific sum under discussion in this context? It lies within the realm of exhibiting kindness while

maintaining utmost honesty. These are the two objectives that you should diligently pursue in your communication endeavors. There are instances of overlapping, as well as instances of non-overlapping occurrences. An individual who consistently prioritizes honesty may not always exhibit kindness, and conversely, a person who demonstrates kindness may not always uphold absolute honesty.

When discussing the concept of honesty and using the phrase "not always completely," we are referring to certain situations where this principle may not universally apply. Typically, falsehood is not the optimal solution. However, opting to formulate a response that refrains from engaging with the inquiry is permissible.

Individuals who possess exceptional aptitude in articulating their thoughts might at times appear somewhat unconventional to our perception. They appear to hold extreme views as they have evidently relinquished any semblance of inhibition in voicing their thoughts, fearlessly expressing their desires and exhibiting unabashed boldness in confronting the world. Frequently, these individuals embody the thoughts we wish to express to ourselves or exemplify the qualities we aspire to possess. These individuals frequently embody unconventional characteristics, including free-spiritedness, affection, and creativity, as they traverse the city's streets.

Individuals who fail to contemplate before uttering their words will exhibit complete transparency in their expressions. They will provide a comprehensive understanding of their message, enabling you to discern the true essence of their thoughts while gaining insight into their character. It is an indisputable reality that embracing openness will inevitably render one susceptible to vulnerabilities. Instead of succumbing to fear in light of this fact, you can choose to embrace it. Gandhi was renowned for his steadfast adherence to the principle of nonviolence. In the event of someone wishing to initiate aggression against him, he would willingly permit it, without engaging in retaliatory actions. In doing so, you provide mankind with an empty canvas onto which they can relentlessly imprint acts of mercilessness. The notion posited that individuals who exhibited utmost nonviolence would serve as a conspicuous testament to the heinous actions committed by merciless individuals, thus assuming the role of exemplars for humanity. Through this action, we strive to tap into the fundamental essence of what is beneficial for the well-being of mankind. By undertaking this action, we are assuming the role of a martyr for benevolence, conveying to a malicious individual, "I am willing to sacrifice my life as your demands would cause my demise if I were to retaliate." This represents the utmost scenario, wherein one's life is jeopardized for expressing their thoughts. Nevertheless, Gandhi's theory on nonviolent resistance offers valuable insights, even when confronted with acts of aggression.

On occasion, an individual's endeavor in their personal growth pertains to exercising greater contemplation prior to verbalizing their thoughts. This pertains to the core principle of honesty, which revolves around the axis of kindness. Integrity should always be accompanied by compassion. This can be attributed to the fact that they are two fundamental principles of great significance.

Uncovering The Sources Of Personal Motivation: A Guide

The method and means to provide such stimulus depend upon possessing not only a functional understanding but also a comprehensive knowledge of your workforce. Effective leaders demonstrate a sincere concern for every individual member within the team, and offer customized encouragement that aligns with the unique needs and aspirations of each individual.

The primary determinant in motivating others is the capacity to effectively impact behavior. The attainment of organizational objectives is contingent upon effectively mobilizing individuals to accomplish predetermined and strategic outcomes. The sustainability of such longevity relies on the exhibition of motivation by team members as well as their ability to retain and be inspired.

So what motivates you?

There is no inherently correct or incorrect motivator, as it is important to bear in mind that the purpose of offering motivation is to exert influence over behavior. These alterations in conduct serve a collective objective or organizational outcome.

As stated previously, nonprofit organizations embody a central ethos, belief, or objective that aligns with their cause. Presenting concrete evidence of progress, favorable transformations, and results serves as the essential impetus for inspiring its individuals.

Below are several primary factors that have an impact on human behavior.

Reward

Offering a mechanism of recompense or encouragement is arguably the most primitive manifestation of motivation we encounter. As individuals during our childhood, we are frequently subjected to the behavioral approach known as the 'carrot and stick' mentality. By conducting oneself in a specific manner, we shall obtain the rewards. Consume your vegetables in their entirety and you shall be rewarded with a delectable dessert.

Please proceed directly to bed, and if you behave appropriately, I shall consider purchasing the toy for you. In adulthood, the approaches have become more sophisticated, although the methodology remains unchanged. If you successfully meet the targets, you will be eligible for additional compensation such as a bonus, salary increase, or promotion, among other benefits.

Outcomes

One significant factor that drives individuals is the observable indication of fulfillment. A significant number of individuals find motivation in observing the outcome achieved. Achieving the desired objectives and results can be a highly gratifying achievement, both on a personal level and from a corporate perspective.

Achieving project success is greatly fulfilling and arguably one of my preferred sources of motivation. The act of acknowledging achievement serves as a significant incentive for numerous individuals, regardless of the manner in which it is expressed, given its substantial motivational impact.

Role - Impact

Leaders possess an inherent drive to exert influence, and frequently find their positions conducive to executing this objective. Although some of the most significant influences in history have operated without an officially recognized position, the majority of us still place more value on titles rather than functions.

There are numerous means by which influence can be attained. In this particular section, it is adequate to recognize that the desire to regulate the conduct of others is frequently accomplished through the utilization of authority. Individuals who regard such a platform as a hierarchical source of influence are frequently driven to advance utilizing its capabilities.

Personal Growth

The purpose of training and development encompasses several aims.

It guarantees coherence and alignment within the organization.

It fosters a climate conducive to personal growth and acts as a recruitment hub, facilitating the transmission of the organization's vision and values.

It offers a rigorous standard for quality management and strategic timelines.

It effectively cultivates talent and integrates it into the long-term growth and development of the organization.

Individuals who possess a inclination to pursue continuous training in specific areas of expertise, demonstrate a fervent dedication towards fortifying their professional prospects, and frequently prioritize personal growth above other motivating factors.

Belonging

Being a component of a collective entity significantly influences the decision-making process regarding the allocation of investment to a particular organization. Undoubtedly, a profound motivator in non-profit organizations is the sense of affiliation.

Being an identifiable component of the overall framework and fulfilling one's role is a considerable source of motivation for numerous individuals. The matter does not concern whether individuals will deploy their skills and talents, but rather the specific location in which they will do so. Offering an inclusive atmosphere surpasses other factors in fostering a sense of belonging.

Fear

In spite of the prevailing culture of political correctness, fear continues to be employed as a means of regulating behavior and influencing outcomes. Frequently, I come across approaches whereby substantial strategies are employed to enhance input and maximize the efforts of employees.

Fear, by itself, is inadequate for exerting control, for in the absence of potential consequences, it remains a superficial motivator. Unsuccessful goals, subpar efficiency or outcomes, delegation of tasks to external sources, economic decline, workforce downsizing, cessation of employment, salary adjustments, and demotion are all employed as catalysts to induce behavioral change.

Love

Finally, it is important to highlight the tremendous power that love holds. The Greeks delineated the concept of love into four distinct categories.

Agápe, Érotic love, Philial affection, Storge love

Regardless of the way in which one experiences love, its motivation is expressed in profound manner. Affection transcends emotion and encompasses action. When an individual acts with authentic concern or affection towards another, it serves as a catalyst for fostering various forms of loyalty and transformative behavioral patterns.

Our receptiveness to love is exemplified more in actions rather than words.

People will go above and beyond, extend their support, allocate resources, uphold, safeguard, and even defend the family vision due to it. The demonstration of loyalty through heartfelt recognition of someone's endeavors encompasses all other forms of motivation.

www.ingramcontent.com/pod-product-compliance
Lightning Source LLC
Chambersburg PA
CBHW050252120526
44590CB00016B/2321